What's YOUR Plan?

To Taylor,
Thank you for
your faith, trust &
confidence.
Best wishes,
James A. DeMeo

James A. DeMeo, M.S.

What's YOUR Plan?

A Step-by-Step Guide to Keep Your Family Safe
During Emergency Situations

Copyright © James A. DeMeo, M.S.
Twitter: @JDeMeo007
http://www.smeeventsecurity.com/

ISBN- Print Version 978-0-9989286-3-0
ISBN- e-Book Version: 978-0-9989286-4-7

November 2017
2nd Print – February 2018

Digi-Tall Media – VicToria Freudiger, Publisher
Margie McCurry – PR and Social Media Assistance
Linda T. Phillips – Design and Photo Assistance

Heather Pendley – Pendley's Pro-Editing
Winning Proof - Michelle Hill, Collaborator

Cover Design and illustrations by MASgraphicarts.com

All rights reserved. No part of this book may be reproduced, stored, or transmitted by any means, whether auditory, graphic, mechanical, or electronic without written permission of both publisher and author, except in the case of brief excerpts used in critical articles and reviews. Unauthorized reproduction of any part of this work is illegal and is punishable by law.

Dedication

My first book was written in honor of two extraordinary women in my life:

My late mother, Margaret Mary Hallissey DeMeo who raised me to be the person I am today. Anyone who knew "Mrs. D" in Port Washington, New York, knew she was one special woman.

I love and miss you, Mom.

The second woman that "What's YOUR Plan" is dedicated to is my lovely wife, Esther. Without her love and support over these past 20 years of marriage, I would not be where I am today.

For that, I love you, Esther.

Table of Contents

Thought Leadership 2.0	vii
Foreword	ix - iv
Introduction	xi - x
Chapter 1: Sports and Entertainment Venues, Special Events	3 - 10
Chapter 2: Malls, Shopping Centers	11 - 18
Chapter 3: Places of Worship-Churches, Synagogues, Temples	19 - 24
Chapter 4: Corporate Workplaces-Potential Workplace Violence	25 - 32
Chapter 5: Colleges and Universities-Higher Education	33 - 44
Chapter 6: Festivals, Carnivals, Street Fairs, Amusement, Water Parks, and Theme Parks	45 - 50
Chapter 7: Movie Theatres	51 - 58
Chapter 8: Recreation, Aquatic & Fitness Centers	67 - 68
Conclusion	69 - 70
Appendix (Words of Wisdom)	71 - 72
Glossary	73 - 76
About the Author	77 - 78
Acknowledgments	79
How to Order/How to Book	80
References	81 - 82

Thought Leadership 2.0

A sign of a true leader is one who does not instill fear but rather creates a heightened sense of awareness through education, training, and professional development. Empowering individuals to know what to do in times of emergencies, places them in the best position to protect themselves and their families. It is all about paying attention to their surroundings, knowing how to go in and get out, if necessary.

The purpose of writing "What's Your Plan" is to help others to begin planning a known (not always obsolete) solution – which can be a most important conversation about being prepared during a crises situation. Being ready, being smart, being safe starts with talking about this with your loved ones.

A pre-planned response starts with having the pre-conversation with your loved ones or those around you. Becoming aware of a plan is all about personal situational awareness and survival. A newer, safer plan for your family, your office, or your sports team, for example, starts today, right now.

Foreword

By Captain Jacques K. Gilbert, Police Captain
Apex, North Carolina Police Department

Having an enjoyable experience with a family member or loved one should never be compromised by fear of an attack by an undetected threat. Whether we are having lunch or dinner at a restaurant, attending a sporting event or visiting vendors at a small-town street festival, personal safety is a responsibility and a priority of the attendee and the event planner. Personal safety is evident as we continue to see horrific attacks on innocent victims in the United States and other places around the world. In fact, as I write this foreword, I, along with fellow Americans, are unsettled by an unimaginable attack on many people attending a concert at a venue in Las Vegas. A gunman opened fire from an elevated position resulting in 58 deaths and nearly 500 people injured.

Professionals are calling this the deadliest shooting massacre in US modern day history. The reality is, many people walk around in public places with minimal awareness or apathy. Safety awareness is often elevated only for a period highlighted by mass media. As these events seemingly are frequent, we may subconsciously become desensitized and overlook the potential impact on our family or community security.

While we may feel it's unfair that we have to be concerned about risks associated with personal and family entertainment, the necessary costs of maintaining safety must be factored into the quality of life equation. However, many people lack the knowledge to address this issue. Individuals who need safety instruction includes: the event planner, mother, father, or caregiver tasked with the responsibility of overlooking events related to those for whom they care.

My 27 years as a law enforcement professional, and church security director, places me in a position to consider personal safety at the forefront daily. Safety planning also applies to my own life when I spend time with family at my residence, restaurants, malls, and other public places. Awareness and personal safety are both important and necessary for my family and me.

The strategies presented in this book by James DeMeo, without question, is a blueprint for planning effective personal safety for anyone. From a student at college to a mother shopping at a local store, James provides a game plan that is both straightforward and realistic to elevate your safety while enjoying life. The professional event planner and police commanders can benefit from this intelligence as well. I believe James' passion as a father and industry-recognized security expert working to improve the safety and quality of life for his fellow man, is both impressive and honorable.

As a Police Captain, I'm urging you to join me in consuming the knowledge presented in this book. I guarantee your confidence will be enhanced while becoming a safety champion for your family and community.

Jacques K. Gilbert, Police Captain, Apex, NC
President of Blue Lights College - Apex, NC
2015 White House Champion of Change Award - President Barack Obama

Introduction

These are indeed most difficult, trying times. The world we find ourselves living in is one filled with conflict and turmoil. The purpose of this book is not to create fear but rather instill a heightened sense of awareness for you and your family.

After having spent 21 years in law enforcement, a noble but dangerous profession, I should know about trying times. As a member of the Nassau County Police Department on Long Island, New York, I responded to countless domestic incident calls, aided cases, house fires, shots fired, a man with a gun, lost and missing children/adults, auto accidents, some with fatalities, and worked the aftermath of 9/11, the Blackout, and Tropical Storm Irene.

Frankly, I would not change my public service career for anything in the world. It was both personally and professionally rewarding in countless ways. The men and women I served with were honorable, hardworking people. All of us wanted to provide the highest level of service to the residents of Nassau County. I take great pride in knowing I made the communities we serve a better place to live. My time on the Force was special, and for that, I am most thankful.

Since retiring from law enforcement in 2011, I earned a master's degree in sport management from Adelphi University as I embarked on my second career.

Fast forward the clock six years. I am now blessed to be recognized as a subject matter expert both domestically and internationally in Event Security. My mission with writing this book began with a personal experience I had with my family at a suburban shopping mall in Durham, North Carolina in late April 2017.

My being able to formulate my expertise along with my thoughts into a written manuscript happened as a result of my meeting Michelle Hill, Founder of Winning Proof. Although I was still living in Texas, our first venture together happened when in June 2015 with us working on LinkedIn together.

Our moving to North Carolina in March 2017, provided the perfect opportunity for Michelle and I to meet one another in person and craft this book together.

I am excited to share my thoughts and insight with you, my readers, about what actions you and your family can take in times of a crisis.

Thank you for allowing me into your world as I communicate with you on how to keep your family safe during various public situations you may encounter.

The legacy I wish to leave my family and this world is all about my love of public service, being a servant leader, trying to make the world a better, safer place by empowering families to not fear but rather be prepared with the situational awareness to survive the unknown and the unthinkable.

What's YOUR Plan?

Chapter 1

Sports & Entertainment Venues

Just about everyone loves sports. Baseball is our national pastime. We live in a sports-crazed society. Games are now being streamed on social media platforms like Twitter. Today's sports and entertainment industries are multi-billion-dollar juggernauts. With that said, let me pose the following questions:

How many times have you seen videos on YouTube, Facebook, and Instagram where people do crazy things while attending sporting events? If not the intoxicated fan, it's the fence jumper or court stormer. You name it; people can do rather bizarre things while out at the ballpark. Maybe they are just looking for their 15 minutes of fame. But what often happens when we see something perilous taking place?

The guard at the Paris Stadium bombing a few years ago had about ten years in the security industry. Ironically, he never worked the venue before that fateful day. Thankfully, he brought his A-game to work that day and saved many lives, only because he was paying attention to his surroundings.

When you – or you and your family are out in public, do you pay attention to the world around you?

What do you think about while attending a sporting event? You probably have your smartphone out looking for the app that will tell you how long the lines are at the concession stands or the, women's restroom, where to buy merchandise, and all the other bells and whistles. It's all good stuff. Having these things and special booths are what the fan experience is all about. Fan engagement and up to date technology make for a winning combination. A sports marketer's dream.

I get it. But what happens at the game if someone is looking to make their mark for all the wrong reasons? You are sitting comfortably in your seat in section 101 alongside your wife and kids, and life is good. You work hard, really hard. You are enjoying that ice-cold beer on a hot summer day. No doubt you should enjoy yourself. You paid good money for your seats and expect to be entertained safely and securely.

Here are some thoughts that you may consider the next time you venture out to the ballpark:

1. Do you remember where you parked your vehicle?

2. If you took mass transit, can you recall which subway/train or bus station will bring you back home?

3. Which entrance did you use to enter the stadium? Gate number?

4. Did you check your smart phone weather app before you left for the stadium?

5. If you drove your vehicle, did you have a full tank of gas, flashlight with working batteries, and a roadside emergency kit?

6. Do you plan on getting out of the venue early to beat the crowds?

7. Did you discuss a pre-planned meeting spot for you and your family if you were to get separated?

8. Can you recall the clothing description your 8-year-old son/daughter was wearing if he/she was to wander away from you?

9. Do you remember the location of the parking garage where you parked your vehicle?

10. Do you have cash, photo ID, credit/debit card in your wallet or purse?

11. Is your cellphone/smartphone fully charged?

12. Do you have bottled water in your vehicle?

These are some thoughts to consider before you go out to the ballpark. With the advances in modern technology, professional sports entities do an excellent job properly screening patrons as fans make their way into the stadium. What about the stadium, venues, and arenas that may not have the same resources as the professional ranks?

Knowing (remembering) which direction you entered the venue and how you may need to get out in the case of an actual emergency is vital for surviving a critical event. It is always advised to follow the direction of assigned law enforcement working the venue.

I would suggest reviewing the above list and having the conversation with your family to discuss each and every point/question until you feel there will be an automatic response by each member of your family, staff, or team.

Practice, Practice, Practice

Sports & Entertainment Venues:

Personal Mindset: Situational awareness, survival.

What's YOUR Plan?

Potential Challenges: Active Shooter, workplace violence, drones, IED/bomb scares, inclement/severe weather, chemical/radiological/biological attack, terrorism, lone wolf, domestic/international terrorist, protests, riots, civil unrest at or near open-ended stadiums, intoxicated or belligerent fans.

Key Points: Having a well-thought-out pre-planned response for your family makes perfect sense. The challenges we see in today's society are not going away anytime soon. Be prepared, always increase your knowledge, and maintain vigilance. The name of the game is survival.

Question: What's Your Plan?

Exercise Action List:

☐ 1. Talk about the last sporting event you attended, this way things are still fresh in your mind.

☐ 2. Visit your favorite team's website and read the link about "codes of conduct."

Chapter 1

☐ 3. Make your checklist and share your thoughts with one another to measure your progress. Remember, your plan is simply your plan – discover what works best for you and your loved ones.

☐ 4. Designate a special meeting place for you and your family. If you have a unique "code word," keep it to just you and your family.

☐ 5. Take time to review steps one through four.

Chapter 2

Malls, Shopping Centers

Retail Loss Prevention

Let's face it: We all love to shop until the bills conveniently show up in our mailbox, of course. In the security world, shopping malls and retail outlets are considered "soft targets" which essentially mean they are easily penetrated targets due to the openness of the environment. Many of today's retailers partner with contract security companies; some armed and unarmed personnel to act as an extra set of eyes and ears for the property manager. You may see a jewelry store with higher priced items contract with local law enforcement, having an armed officer protecting the tenant's inventory.

As mentioned earlier, shopping centers are free open spaces. There are usually no metal detectors or screening measures as you enter the mall. You will see mall security walking throughout the space, or riding on Segways and driving motor patrol vehicles in the exterior parking lots. Security does this as a means of being proactive in their crime deterrence duties. Many department stores hire undercover loss prevention officers who keep a watchful eye for shoplifters and credit card fraud.

With that being said, here are some helpful suggestions and questions you may ask yourself before you and your family head out to the shopping mall:

1. When you arrived at the mall, did the garage area have proper lighting?

2. What's the location of the guest services kiosk? They are the mall greeters for the property manager. If you have a security need, they can immediately contact security personnel.

3. Look around for uniformed law enforcement, especially during the peak holiday shopping season, which usually runs from Black Friday/Thanksgiving through New Year's Day. Make sure to let the officers know if anything or anybody looks suspicious to you.

4. Did you remember the exact parking location of your vehicle?

5. Try to stay together as a family/group. There is always strength in numbers.

6. At all times stay aware of your surroundings and look around for suspicious individuals, especially when first exiting your vehicle.

7. If the lights were to go out in the mall, have you discussed a pre-planned meeting location with your family? It could happen with a facility-related issue such as a brownout, or when a transformer goes out in the surrounding area.

8. Look around you as you are walking throughout the mall. Many shoppers tend to look down at their smartphones. The bad guys know to look for the distracted shopper. Don't

become the victim of a shoplifter or purse snatcher. Protect yourself and your property. Be observant of your surroundings at all times. Hold your purse, secure your wallet, and keep your personal belongings close to your body. Place valuable items inside a generic shopping bag – you don't need to show the world you just purchased a fancy Mac Book Pro or expensive jewelry. Make sure you and your property make it home safely.

9. If you see a child or elderly person walking around, one who appears lost or separated from their family, notify security immediately. Chances are, security is searching for the same individual.

10. Look for egress areas, exit points in case of a true emergency, e.g., fire, bomb scare, active shooter situation. Always follow directions from law enforcement.

11. Visit the property manager's website, follow them on Twitter, and know store hours and location, acquire important contact numbers and updates in the event of closures, emergency notifications, and evacuations.

12. Avoid wearing loose-fitting clothing or sandals that may get caught in escalators.

13. If you are in the food court area and see a wet spill, notify facilities, housekeeping, janitorial or security. There's nothing worse than to see a wet spill, not tell anyone and then someone falls and gets injured. You would want someone else to do the same for you or your family member. You really can make a difference by pointing out things that are out of place or do not seem as they should. Don't be shy; instead let someone know, and you will feel really good afterward. It's simply the right thing to do.

14. When leaving the mall, pay close attention to who is around as you make your way towards your vehicle. Be confident when you walk, square your shoulders. The bad guys look for any weakness they can find. Have your cellphone out and ready to call 911, if necessary. This is not a fear-based approach, rather it's you simply being best prepared. When you are paying attention, the bad guys won't be paying attention to you. Don't be a victim; stay empowered.

15. Remember to be vigilant and trust your gut instincts. If it does not feel right, it's probably not right. Let the authorities know immediately about any of your safety concerns.

Suburban Durham Shopping Mall - And Then There Was Darkness

In late April 2017, my family and I visited a local shopping mall in Durham, North Carolina. We were shopping in a larger retail anchor store—you know, the big stores that usually help attract shoppers to the mall. We had been there nearly an hour when, all of a sudden, the lights went out in the entire mall. My first thought was that perhaps this was a cyber security/ facilities breach. My 13-year-old son, Aidan, turned to me and said, "Hey, Dad, what are the chances someone could come in here and shoot this place up?" I was awestruck that such a young man, wise beyond his years, could have such a thought process. As they say, "From the mouths of babes."

We left the store a short while later. As we made our way to our car, I remember store security telling us to watch the traffic lights as they were out in all directions. They were right. As we entered our vehicle, cars were exiting the exterior parking lots with all the traffic lights in the surrounding area having absolutely no power. This scene was eerily reminiscent of my work with the Nassau County Police Department during the Blackout of August 2003 that hit the New York area.

What I remember most about the experience at the mall was that many shoppers continued to look down at their smartphones, completely oblivious to what all was happening around them. It still amazes me to this day, with all that's happened in the world, that some people still choose to live in a bubble, desensitized to what may happen.

Thankfully, that night all went well as we made our way home. I initially looked at my gas gauge in my rather fuel-efficient vehicle and noticed that we had about a half a tank of gas. My next thoughts went to my experiences living through Hurricane Sandy on Long Island. Gas was tough to come by during the early aftermath of the worst storm to hit Long Island in nearly 100 years. The experience at the mall was a real *eye-opener*. As soon as I could, I pulled into a gas station and topped off the tank. You know me, I am not taking any chances.

Later that evening, we sat down as a family and began talking about our mall experience. Everyone engaged in a conversation, a timely one, while the events were still fresh in our minds. We talked about creating a plan for our family on what to do if the unimaginable were to happen while out shopping at the mall. Our family discussion sparked the impetus for this book, all starting with my son's view of the world that we find ourselves living in today. The evening eventually became quite powerful, to say the least.

Chapter 3

Places of Worship

Churches, Synagogues, Temples

When attending your place of worship, it's important to remember that most churches are open to the public. There are usually no metal detectors to pass through, as it's considered a relatively safe place to bring your family. However, due to the ongoing instability throughout the Middle East and other parts of the world, securing places of worship is garnering more attention. Being prepared and having a preplanned response is key when confronted with an adverse situation.

    Here are some helpful suggestions to take into consideration while attending your place of worship.

1. Watch the news and keep up with current events around the world. Is your place of worship one that might be targeted by unscrupulous individuals? Being informed means knowing what to expect in the event that the unthinkable were to occur.

2. Volunteer for your church, mosque, or temple's safety and security team. The church leadership team often holds security briefings and can benefit from your knowledge, especially if you are ex-military or retired law enforcement. Paramedics, MD's, nurses, and healthcare professionals who are parishioners can often help if a fellow member is having a medical crisis.

3. Know the exact location of where the Automated External Defibrillator (AED) is located in your church building. On the other hand, you should know if the church does not have one in case of emergencies. If you have the proper training, you may save someone's life before EMS arrives. Volunteer firefighters can greatly assist in the event of a building fire.

Should this occur, a safe, timely evacuation is critical.

4. Park your vehicle near a well-lit area in the event you are attending an evening service.

5. Follow the directions of the parking lot attendants; most are volunteers. Vehicle safety is essential. No one wants a car wreck or pedestrian struck in the parking lot.

6. Know where the exits are in the event you have to evacuate the building.

7. If you see someone who looks somewhat suspicious around any area of the church, let a church staff member know. Again, churches are free, open spaces. If it does not feel right to you, share that information with a church staff member. It's better to be vigilant than a victim.

8. Churches in some states, like Texas, are enlisting armed security officers on church property. Unfortunately, it's the world we live in these days.

9. If you observe that any exterior parking lot lighting fixtures have gone out, let the church facilities staff know.

10. If you see a wet spill near the water fountains or in the restrooms, let housekeeping know, or

try to clean up the area the best you can. No one wants to end up going to the hospital because they slipped on wet flooring.

Places of Worship:

Personal Mindset: Be mindful of suspicious individuals.

Potential Challenges: Active shooter, bomb scare, fire, workplace violence, terrorism, inclement weather conditions.

Key Points: Be vigilant, be knowledgeable, be prepared, and pay attention to what's going on around you. Share information with church staff members

Question: What's Your Plan?

Exercise Action List:

☐ 1. Meet with your pastor or church leader and discuss any safety/security concerns.

☐ 2. Get involved in the process. Invite law enforcement, fire department, EMS, and security consultants to tour your place of worship. The more knowledge first responders have, the better they are prepared in their response.

☐ 3. Start or join your security leadership team; share information and knowledge.

☐ 4. Conduct safety drills at your parish, mosque, temple or church. Being prepared means being in the best position possible to survive a critical event.

☐ 5. Take time to review steps one through four.

Chapter 4

Corporate Workplaces

Potential Workplace Violence Occurrences

A Note to Employers:

Lead from the front. Don't instill fear, but rather empower your employees to be best prepared when tragedy strikes. Invest in your staff and equip them with the necessary tools to survive the unimaginable. Having a proactive security mindset begins with training, fire drills, dry runs, computer simulations, threat and behavioral analysis, situational awareness, workplace and Active Shooter awareness training, and responsible social media monitoring. This applies to every security industry vertical.

Lead from the Front — Train Today — Train Now

How many of us are fortunate enough to work remotely with our employers? No doubt it's a great gig. Working from home has many advantages, but for the rest of us who have to make the trek into the office, the 9-5 grind, the gig has some potential disadvantages. With that said, let's take a look at the most recent stats on workplace violence.

According to the Department of Homeland Security, here's a look at what you should be watching for in a potential Active Shooter in your workplace.

> PROFILE OF AN ACTIVE SHOOTER: An Active Shooter is an individual actively engaged in killing or attempting to kill people in a densely populated area; in most cases, Active Shooter's use firearm(s), and there is no pattern or method to their

Chapter 4

selection of victims. Active Shooter situations are unpredictable and evolve quickly. Typically, the immediate deployment of law enforcement is required to stop the shooting and mitigate harm to victims. Because Active Shooter situations are often over within 10 to 15 minutes, before law enforcement arrives on the scene, individuals must be prepared both mentally and physically to deal with an Active Shooter situation.

Quite sobering, right? In all fairness, law enforcement does a terrific job when confronted with these types of scenarios. But the issue is: how can you best survive before the good guys get to your workplace if faced with a workplace violence situation? It's those crucial first 10-15 minutes we will attempt to address as far as your personal safety.

Here are some helpful suggestions you can utilize while at the office.

1. Personal situation awareness. Pay attention to your workplace, the people who enter it, and your surroundings. It makes sense to remain

vigilant by looking around and making certain you notice your surroundings.

2. If something or someone does not seem right, trust your gut instincts. If a situation does not appear normal – trust your instincts. It's not that you are paranoid, it's that you are hyper-vigilant. Your safety and that of your coworkers are key.

3. Run, Hide, Fight and "See Something, Say Something" is always a good way to go.

4. Let your immediate supervisor know about an overly troubled co-worker. You are not snitching. It's simply the right thing to do.

5. If someone you don't know attempts to enter a restricted area, ask them if they need assistance. Let security know about your interactions with any strangers. Don't allow anyone to follow in behind you. Don't let unknown persons use your access card. If you don't know the person, simply question who they are. Don't assume they are there for the same reasons you are.

6. Know the physical layouts of your own workspace. Take particular note of entrances/exits; how to get out in the event of a violent situation.

7. Get to know your workplace security officer. They have the most current information and can be a great asset for sharing information with law enforcement, if need be. Many of these officers are former law enforcement or ex-military and have years of experience. Thank them for their diligence in helping to keep your workplace safe.

8. Volunteer to become a part of your organization's safety/security team; this is a shared responsibility. Working in independent silos, thinking that security is another person's job, is a shortsighted view in today's challenging times. Take a vested interest in your own personal safety. Get involved in the process. It's a win-win scenario.

9. If you see an access door not working properly, for instance, the light is green when it should be red for closed, tell facilities/security to correct the condition. Don't assume they have already been notified.

10. You're exiting your vehicle in the company parking lot, and you see a suspicious/possibly homeless person. Walk confidently, square your shoulders, and look all around you. Be safe and proceed to the office. Notify security staff immediately.

Corporate Workplaces:

Personal Mindset: Survival. Be vigilant, share information with your supervisor and security staff.

Potential Challenges: Active Shooter, workplace violence occurrence.

Key Points: Education, training, knowledge, sharing information is key.

Question: What's Your Plan?

Chapter 4

Exercise Action List:

☐ 1. Contact your immediate supervisor and ask them what your workplace violence plan may be.

☐ 2. Meet with security director and discuss how you can have a more active role as a team leader.

☐ 3. Practice dry runs, tabletop exercises, evacuation drills, and computer simulations to be best prepared in the event a workplace violence situation were to occur.

☐ 4. Roleplay scenarios with fellow coworkers on what to do if this were to occur in your workplace.

☐ 5. Be involved in the process. It's all about your safety and those of your coworkers. Be safe, be smart.

Chapter 5

Centers of Learning

Colleges, Universities & Public Libraries

Many of us have children attending college and we're well aware that properly securing today's colleges and universities has its challenges. Current economic conditions that exist, commencing with the Great Recession of 2008, are partly due to the burdensome student loan debt quandary many families are currently facing today. College presidents make tremendous efforts and take great strides in safeguarding their university's brand to protect their bottom line.

As an example of amassing endowment wealth, Harvard University's endowment for the fiscal year 2014 was 36.4 billion dollars. Another challenge worth consideration has been the emergence of online education hybrid-learning and its relative impact on the brick and mortar world of higher education.

Furthermore, fierce competition exists to attract the best of the sharpest minds, not to mention the most gifted student-athletes, to increase enrollments. Along with this competition comes an excessive price tag, not only for the university itself, but also the prospective students and their parents. Tuition, room and board, textbooks, lab, and student fees are all costs associated with attending today's colleges and universities. From an operations/facilities standpoint, the economic costs are quite staggering.

Let us take a look:

Economic Facts and Statistics:

According to a 1995 study conducted by College and Planning:

> Colleges and universities in the US spent a staggering $6.1 billion annually on associated construction costs. By 2006,

these costs skyrocketed to $15 billion. Post-recession 2008, spending costs slightly decreased, but since the year 2013, associated costs reached $10.9 billion.

According to a study conducted by the National Center for Education Statistics:

> Students ranging in ages from 18-24 experienced enrollment increases by 3.1 percent. An increase in the student enrollment population necessitated a need to build more dorms and student classrooms. Let's further explore where the accelerated spending spree has driven the market.

A Call to Arms: Build It and They Will Come:

We have seen a proverbial arms race concerning upgraded facility construction at colleges and universities throughout the U.S. Furthermore, higher education entities have spent billions of dollars expanding their facilities. Upgrading atriums, mezzanines, gymnasiums, indoor tracks, locker rooms, aquatic centers, racquetball, squash courts, as well as enhanced training facilities, college recreation centers strive to improve socialization among their students.

They do this to promote fitness and active, healthy lifestyles.

    Intramural sports and sports clubs serve as means for students to stay connected with the university, thereby enhancing the overall college experience. This connection further serves as a means for students to grow both personally and professionally. Membership costs exist for fitness, swimming, and racquetball classes. College recreation centers offer membership packages to community members and university alumni.

    Regarding spending on upgraded facilities, the University of Iowa boasts a fifty-three-million-dollar recreation center. Texas Tech University in Lubbock has access to a water park. On the security front, Long Beach State packs a powerful punch in the facilities game with their seventy-million-dollar health and wellness center in addition to its utilization of hand scanners for access control measures.

    For many years, the asset protection discipline has been viewed as being reactionary in nature. There's no question; we live in troubling times. With the instability in the Middle East to the advent of the Boston Marathon bombing, Virginia Tech, Columbine, and the Newton, Connecticut, Las Vegas, and Sutherland Springs, TX shootings, security challenges remain constant and are prevalent in today's society.

When discussing how to secure the higher education vertical, proper recognition of specific threats and vulnerabilities currently exist which present significant challenges. The stakeholders include law enforcement, first responders, EMS, paramedics, college public safety teams, students, faculty, and administrators. The need to adequately protect lives and safeguard assets is part and parcel to ensuring a safe and protective learning environment.

Challenges such as workplace violence, Active Shooters, IED-bomb scare/suspicious packages, drones, lone wolf, domestic incidents, theft, burglary, arson, criminal mischief, sexual assaults, public intoxication, drug abuse, Title IX and Cleary Act compliance standards exist in this environment.

How Best to Protect Students and Safeguard the University's Brand:

1. Colleges/Universities: Due to existing challenges, it's imperative for college administrators to maintain precise and efficient lines of communication with their Public Safety teams. Examples such as access control, credentialing, physical security, biometrics, ingress/egress/effective screening methods, especially during on-campus sporting events,

concerts, and fundraisers, best help to mitigate risk and keep the environment safe and secure.

2. Event Management – On Campus Sporting Events: The last thing any university president wants is a security breach on his/her campus. The need to work with the risk management component of the organization is also a worthwhile endeavor. Educating your housekeeping, public safety, and student volunteer staff about slips, trips, and falls, intoxicated students/guests, and prohibited tailgating in campus stadium parking lots makes for proactive security/risk mitigation initiatives. Also, paying attention to inclement/ hazardous weather conditions and actively monitoring social media platforms such as Facebook, LinkedIn, Twitter, Tumblr, Instagram, and Pinterest, before, during, and post events places security in the best position possible. When creating security omnipresence at events, public safety teams can implement bike safety patrol and foot and mobile patrol unit strategies to monitor existing crowd conditions. Garnering support from local law enforcement, mounted unit-horses and canines for potential crowd control/bomb threat challenges makes perfect sense.

Chapter 5

The NCS4-National Center for Spectator Sports Safety & Security (NCS4.com) affiliated with the University of Southern Mississippi has been proactive in creating educational resources, and career development security staff entrusted with safe-guarding today's college sporting events.

Furthermore, public safety teams can offer the following training and resources for its students, faculty and staff members: Social networking security, safety alerts, emergency preparedness, cold/warm weather tips, emergency evacuations, anti-theft tips, sexual assault awareness, hurricane preparedness, student escorts to and from classrooms and dormitories, safe dating and mobile device connectivity in true emergency situations where the University Mass Notification System is required/ activated.

1. On-Campus Recreation/Fitness Centers: Safety and security challenges along with threats and vulnerabilities exist in this type of environment. The need for staff to be properly vetted and receive proper background checks places ownership groups in a position of strength. Also, efficient screening methods should be implemented with patrons/guests. Additional physical measures such as credentialing and access control should be utilized as well. Additionally, a periodic review of SOP's (standard operating procedure and security

protocols) should be tweaked as often as is practical. Keeping the lines of communication open when first responders place public safety initiatives is at the forefront of any effective security initiative.

2. An example of a security challenge occurred in April 2015 on the campus of Washington State University. Student Dmitry Dementyev made verbal threats indicating that he had plans on detonating a bomb inside the college recreation center. WSU police responded, deemed the situation/area safe, and placed the student under arrest, charging him with felony harassment. The student subsequently received mental health treatment.

Public Libraries:

When was the last time you visited your local public library to check out books, cd's, or videos? When you arrived at the information desk, did everything appear normal around you? More likely than not, things were going just fine. But what if something unusual were to happen? Do you know your libraries exit locations?

In summary, the significance for security staff members in the higher education and recreation

Chapter 5

centers space is ongoing. Challenges continuously exist. These are troubling times, and now is no time to be complacent, thinking it won't happen to you. Knowledge creates power. Being proactive with regard to your security places you in a position of strength. An entrusted duty of care exists for all those acting within the parameters of public safety initiatives. Public safety teams conducting threats and vulnerability assessments for your stadium, venue, arena, recreation facility, or performing arts center is part and parcel of providing a safe, secure and enjoyable college environment.

Here are some safety and security suggestions to use the next time you visit your child, grandchild, loved one, etc., attending a college or university. These tips also apply when visiting your local public library.

1. Pay close attention to your surroundings. Vigilance is critical.

2. Check the university website for school closings, crisis communication, public safety information, and severe weather warnings. Being: "in the know" is a good place to be.

3. If employed by a university, look to join the public safety team in some capacity. Team

leaders are always needed and help to foster communications with law enforcement.

4. If confronted with an Active Shooter situation, "Run, Hide, Fight", is a good way to go. Follow directions from first responders.

5. When parking your vehicle on campus, ensure your vehicle is in a well-lit area, especially at night.

6. If you are a student walking from class and feel unsafe, contact public safety for an escort.

7. If you are a student on campus, look for the location of emergency call boxes.

8. Know where the student services and public safety offices are located on campus.

9. If you see any suspicious activity in the parking lots, notify public safety as soon as possible. Libraries typically employ security officers. Share information with security, especially with matters of your personal safety.

10. If you see someone launching a drone on or near campus, notify public safety and they will investigate depending on the circumstances and their school policy.

Again, this information has been a broad overview of what to do, how to react, and what to expect on a college campus, university, or your local public library, should something out of the ordinarily occur. Check the public safety office to become familiar with the do's and don'ts of the university policy.

When visiting the public library, stop by the information desk if you have any concerns.

Campus security's function is to provide your child a safe and enjoyable educational experience. The more information public safety has from the university's student body, their family, and faculty, the better overall security environment.

Chapter 6

Festivals, Carnivals, Street Fairs, Theme Parks

Who doesn't love going to a community street fair? Whether you live in a small rural town or a large urban center, venturing out, especially on the weekend, can be especially fun for the entire family. Arts and crafts, classic automobiles, exotic antiques, balloon rides, cotton candy, and the best organic coffee you can drink. You are sure to find what you're looking for during your family outing.

Post Manchester, we see numerous challenges around the globe. Terrorist and anti-government groups thrive on the innocent and vulnerable when launching potential attacks. 'Confined space

What's YOUR Plan?

protection' is a term used to describe the proper safeguarding of densely populated areas.

Being aware of your surroundings, especially when you're with your loved ones, makes perfect sense, doesn't it? Below are some helpful tips for you and your family to follow the next time you attend a local festival, carnival, or street fair:

1. Take a look at the event website before leaving your home. Look for the best time to arrive, parking locations, ingress/egress routes, and weather conditions, especially when outdoors.

2. Make sure your vehicle has a full tank of gas and is in good working condition. It always pays to stay ahead of your vehicle maintenance schedule. Not a plug for your local mechanic, but who wants the hassle of a car breakdown, dead battery, or flat tire? Even in town, any unexpected car maintenance is a drag.

3. Upon arrival, follow parking attendants or police instructions on where to park. Look for proper signage and lighting as you arrive at the lot.

4. Remember where you parked your vehicle. Take a photo on your cellphone if necessary. Some newer vehicles have a locator app which you can download. Technology is great. Use it to your advantage.

5. Carry a flashlight in your vehicle if visibility is poor at night. Use your cellphone flashlight when walking back to your car after the event if lighting conditions are poor. Don't walk in the street – you risk getting hit by a car.

6. Look for the presence of local law enforcement at the event. It always pays to know where the good guys are at the festival.

7. While at the festival, look for a tent to cool down inside of – if warmer weather conditions prevail. Drink plenty of water. Staying hydrated is healthy and smart.

8. Wear a medical ID bracelet if you suffer from any life-threatening conditions. In the event of a medical emergency, paramedics will need to know of any existing medical conditions you may have.

9. Grasp your small children by the hand. Talk with your little ones beforehand about not wandering off, and warn them about not talking to strangers. A discussion is not meant to scare your children, but to rather educate them about stranger danger safety. It's worth your time (and theirs) to be educated and empowered.

10. Discuss a predetermined meeting place in the event of an evacuation, hurricane, tornado, errant drone, fire, Active Shooter, terrorist attack, a bomb scare. Have that talk; being empowered goes hand in hand with knowledge. Always follow law enforcement instructions in the event of an actual emergency.

Chapter 6

Festivals, Carnivals, Street Fairs, Theme Parks

Personal Mindset: Be aware of your surroundings.

Potential Challenges: Active Shooter, bomb scare, fires, drones, terrorism, stampede, inclement/severe weather conditions.

Key Points: Awareness, safety, and security pre-planning is key. Have the family discussion before venturing out to the carnival.

Question: What's Your Plan?

Exercise Action List:

☐ 1. Before you venture out to the festival, check social media platforms and the festival website to see if there are any emergency updates.

☐ 2. Go over your meeting place plan.

Decide your code word in the event a true emergency occurs.

What's YOUR Plan?

☐ 3. Pay attention to the location of the first aid tent, law enforcement, and first responders' location at the event.

☐ 4. Know exactly which gate you entered and the location of where you parked your vehicle. Be safe and have fun.

Note: The same strategies can be applied when venturing out to an amusement or theme park. The only big difference is you will probably be outdoors. Just remember to be aware of any inclement weather conditions, i.e., hurricanes, tornados, flash floods, blizzards, dense fog, or torrential storms before heading out to the park. There are some terrific weather apps, just go ahead and download them. Technology works great when you use it. Don't play the guessing game. Be prepared in advance, have a plan. Enjoy the rides and don't forget the cotton candy.

Chapter 7

Movie Theatres/Cinemas

Pass me the popcorn and a large Coke. Time to relax in those extra-large comfortable reclining leather chairs. Today's movie theatres have humongous screens, Wi-Fi; all the bells and whistles of a luxury movie-going experience. Who wants to stay at home when you can watch your favorite actor on the big screen? Venturing out to your local movie theatre is generally considered a safe proposition, and you can't beat matinees for the best ticket prices. But what happens if your worst nightmare unfolds, not so much on the screen, but rather, inside the theatre?

What's YOUR Plan?

    As we look back to midnight, July 20, 2012, at the Century 16 movie theatre shooting in Aurora, Colorado, the shooter caused mayhem when he slipped into the theatre and killed many innocent people and injured countless others on that fateful night. Earlier, the shooter had purchased a ticket to the show and slipped out an emergency exit unnoticed. He went to his car and brought back an arsenal of weapons and used them to kill innocent people inside the theatre. Unless you happen to be an off-duty police officer, how could you possibly survive such an onslaught of terror?

    One such organization dedicated to movie safety and security is the National Organization of Theatre Owners. This group, based in Washington, DC and North Hollywood, CA, looks to unify cinemas all over the world. One aspect of their business operations model is online staff training modules. Great idea! Proactive staff training is a good way for employees to keep their skills sharp if tragedy strikes.

    Now, it is time to learn how to map out your game plan the next time you head out to the movies.

1. Arrive at the theatre well ahead of the scheduled movie run time to purchase your tickets, unless you have already purchased them online. Planning ahead gives you and

your family a chance to get the fresh popcorn and best seats. Avoiding unnecessary lines means you can settle in and glance over the layout of the theatre and specific screening room.

2. Since you arrived early, that means you scored a great parking spot, right? Also, no rushing means less stress. Give yourself and your family plenty of time to arrive at the show.

3. If the cinema is attached to a large retail mall area, look for security officers and law enforcement patrolling the parking lots. It's great to have the good guys keeping an eye on your vehicle as well as ensuring your safety.

4. Park your vehicle in a well-lit area within close walking distance to the theatre. Don't leave any valuables inside your automobile: such as laptops, cellphones, tablets, documents containing personal information, cash, you name it. Safeguard your property. There's nothing more frustrating than coming out from seeing an epic movie and discovering that your vehicle has been broken into.

5. When you get inside the theatre, look to see where the exits are in case you have to leave during an emergency situation.

6. If someone or something looks suspicious to you, inform the security staff or law enforcement. Make certain to express your concerns. That includes what appears to you to be a suspicious vehicle driving around the lot. Jot down the license plate number and vehicle description. Share this information with mall or theatre security. Don't wait for somebody else to report it.

7. When leaving home, make certain your vehicle has a full tank of gas, has continuously been maintained, and your cellphone is fully charged. A plan such as this just makes good sense. Did I mention keeping a flashlight in your car?

8. If a fellow movie patron becomes loud, obnoxious, or starts creating a disturbance, alert a staff member immediately. Try not to engage the agitated person directly; instead, let security know what's happening. The theatre has a code of conduct with house-specific rules to follow. Refer to the reference

section to read an example from AMC Theatre Code of Conduct: https://cdn.amctheatres.com/Media/Default/PDFs/code-of-conduct-policy.pdf.

9. In the event of an Active Shooter incident, make your plan the "Run, Hide, Fight" strategy for survival.

10. If the theatre is set up with a security app – once downloaded, send an anonymous text about any unusual activity inside the theatre.

Movie Theatres/Cinemas:

Personal Mindset: Look and see what's going on around you.

Potential Challenges: Active Shooter, workplace violence, fire, drug/narcotics usage, intoxicated patrons, fighting, terrorism, civil unrest, bomb scare, inclement weather situation, or protests near or around theatre.

Key Points: Vigilance, situational awareness, "See Something, Say Something."

Question: What's Your Plan?

Exercise Action List:

☐ 1. Before going out the theatre, check their website for any updates.

☐ 2. Once you enter the theatre, know where the exit doors are located.

☐ 3. Escort your children, especially your young ones to the restroom. Don't ever allow your children to wander off unsupervised.

☐ 4. Pay attention to your surroundings. Inform the staff if you see anything is out of the ordinary or suspicious. Now, it's time for that popcorn.

☐ 5. Enjoy the show!

Chapter 8

Recreation/Fitness Centers

    Have you ever worked out at your local YMCA or campus fitness center? People who enjoy working out do so for many reasons, some being mental clarity, improved mood, and overall enhanced physical/cardiovascular fitness. With that said, when was the last time you worked out and were concerned about your safety? Typically, fitness centers are generally considered safe, secure places to work up a sweat, socialize, take a class, and meet up with a friend or neighbor.

What's YOUR Plan?

However, due to many challenges we have seen throughout the world, it pays to be vigilant and aware of your surroundings, and this even includes going to the gym.

Some concerns to be aware of are as follows:

1. Unauthorized entry of unscrupulous persons
2. Theft of personal belongings
3. Criminal mischief to automobiles
4. Fire
5. Bomb scare
6. Active Shooter, possible workplace violence scenario
7. Natural disaster, inclement weather, sheltering in place vs. evacuation

Now that you have this handbook and have plans to read and study it, you may want to review some of the following safety and security tips the next time you go the gym. Note: This applies to both male and female patrons, based upon your comfort level.

1. Review the company website for safety and security contact information and procedures

before going to or joining the gym. Awareness and knowledge are powerful tools to ensure your own personal safety.

2. Park your vehicle or bike in a well-observed location of the lot so that security staff can see your property. They will help prevent any potential theft while in the center.

3. Have your keys out, and cellphone available as you walk to and from your car. Travel with a buddy/workout pal, if possible. Walking in groups is always a good tip to follow. There is always strength in numbers.

4. Grab your small children by the hand as you exit from your car and go into the center. Sometimes, people don't follow driving rules in parking lots. You do not want your child wandering into oncoming traffic. Let's avert a potential tragedy from ever happening.

5. When leaving anywhere at night, walk along a well-lit path towards your vehicle. Do not text while you're walking to your car! Predators

What's YOUR Plan?

look for distracted people, especially females. Plus, you could trip and fall.

6. If you feel somewhat uneasy about your safety, request that the center's security staff escort you to your vehicle. If you are on a college campus, ask public safety/campus police to escort you to your dormitory, classroom, or vehicle.

7. Have a pre-planned response discussion with your family/friends before going to the gym. If there is an emergency, discuss a central meeting place if your family is working out in a different area of the center. Always follow directives from security and law enforcement.

8. If you see someone in the parking lot or around the lobby looking suspicious or disoriented, inform the staff of your concerns. The individual may also be having a medical emergency – tell someone. Help them and this will help you as well.

Chapter 8

9. While in the gym, look for all the entrance/exit signs just in case you have to evacuate quickly from the building.

10. Don't permit anyone you don't know to follow you into a secured access area. You have a key fob or access card for a reason. Security staff knows who you are based on your photo and paid membership. If the unknown person says to you that they forgot theirs, ask them politely to check with the staff at the front desk. This precaution is for everyone's safety. I am all about being courteous, but not at the expense of personal safety.

11. If you see someone driving suspiciously in the parking lot, take down the vehicle license plate/tag number and share that information with the local authorities. That includes if the person is on foot; try to remember physical description, clothing items, unique markers such as a backpack, hat, fancy or distinctive writing/labels on their clothing.

12. Be safe, have fun, and enjoy yourself at the gym. Just be aware of what's going on around you. If you have any concerns, let someone in authority know.

Recreation/Fitness Centers:

Personal Mindset: Pay attention to your surroundings.

Potential Challenges: Active Shooter, bomb scare, fire, improvised explosive devices (IED), inclement/severe weather conditions, terrorism, civil unrest/protests at or near your gym, workplace violence occurrences.

Key Points: Vigilance, awareness, safety, and security.

Question: What's Your Plan?

Exercise Action List:

☐ 1. Have a pre-planned safety and security discussion with your family.

☐ 2. Check out the gym's website for any updates you many need to know about.

☐ 3. Pay close attention to the location entrance/exits in case you have to quickly evacuate the building.

☐ 4. Ask to see where the first aid office is in the event you or a family member needs medical assistance.

☐ 5. Have a great workout while you work up a sweat.

Post Event Trauma:
What Do We Tell Our Children?

When tragic events unfold, not only do we deal with the loss of life and the injured, but also the psychological impact felt by those left behind. Post-Columbine, Virginia Tech, Sandy Hook, Manchester, Nice, Paris, Brussels, the Pulse, Sutherland Springs, TX, and Las Vegas, our children's mental health can be dramatically altered by such horrific occurrences. The need for mental health triage and counseling, especially during the early aftermath of a crises situation, cannot be underscored.

We need to take the time to help heal the pain, grief, and suffering that can result from such tragic events. If someone you know needs assistance, help them anyway you possibly can. They are counting on us. Please take the time to visit the following link: https://www.tipoflasvegas.org/about for more information on how to talk to your children.

Conclusion

We are all living in a fast-paced, ever-changing, conflicted world. Social media and technology come at us from many angles, and the need and speed for the way the world is changing cannot be underscored. The need to be equipped with necessary tools for being situationally aware and safety-prepared for the unthinkable is key when confronting the numerous challenges, we face.

As I stated in the introduction, my purpose for writing my first book is not to create fear, but unfortunately, a ton of fear and uncertainty currently exists in our society. Fearful situations are happening more often than most of us would have ever believed. There is also a prevailing thought that *bad things happen to other people, not me*. That's a short-sighted view because it truly is hard to predict other people's actions, but we can learn to pick up clues and indicators. Every one of us should pay attention to them with the best of our ability.

Knowledge and education bring empowerment. I have provided you what I believe are some useful tools for your own personal safety toolbox. Keep them at home, at work, or perhaps in your vehicle. These useful tips will help you and your family experience increased awareness in the event you are confronted with a difficult, perhaps life-threatening

What's YOUR Plan?

situation. I am honored and humbled that you have allowed me to become part of your lives, to hear my voice to prepare you during these difficult times.

    Please remember to help one another, as we are all in this together. Remember to share information with one another on a community Facebook page, neighborhood watch, and of course, with law enforcement. Be safe. Be smart. Be prepared.

Thank You,

James A. DeMeo, M.S.

Appendix A

Words of Wisdom

Knowledge is, without question, power. The best way to combat fear is through education and preparation in the event a tragedy strikes. Having a pre-planned response will help you and your family. Now is the time to take the necessary steps to ensure your own personal safety, and it all starts with having a plan.

The question now becomes:

What's YOUR Plan?

Glossary

Anarchy: If you describe a situation as anarchy, it means that nobody seems to be paying any attention to rules or laws.

Civil Unrest: Fighting between different groups of people living in the same country, and losses caused by this fighting are usually not covered by insurance.

Computer Simulation: An event, process, or scenario that is created on a computer.

Confined Space Protection: a term used to describe the proper safeguarding of densely populated areas. http://optimumsecuritypros.com/security-services-houston/event-security/sporting-event-security/ source confined space protection for sporting events.

Drone: Type of aircraft that is pilotless and radio-controlled used for reconnaissance or bombing.

Duty of Care: The legal obligation to safeguard others from harm while they are in your care, using your services, or exposed to your activity.

Egress: The act of going out or forth (or into the world); emergence, departure.

Evacuation: The act of being evacuated; to remove persons from (a city, town, building, area, etc.) for reasons of safety.

First Responder: A person who is trained to provide basic life support in a medical emergency.

IED: A simple bomb that is made and used by someone who is not in the military, often using materials that are not usually used for making bombs. IED is an abbreviation for "improvised explosive device."

Ingress: The act of entering, enter opening.

Metal detector: A device that gives an audible or visual signal when its search head comes close to a

Glossary

metallic object embedded in food, buried in the ground, etc.

Planning: The process of deciding in detail how to do something before you actually start to do it.

Preparation: The process of getting something ready for use or for a particular purpose, or making arrangements for something.

Protest: The act of announcing or showing publicly that you object to something.

Risk Management: The skill or job of deciding what the risks are in a particular situation and taking action to prevent or reduce them.

Safety: The state of being safe from harm or danger.

Security: Refers to all the measures that are taken to protect a place, or to ensure that only people with permission enter or leave it.

SOP: Standard Operating Procedure.

What's YOUR Plan?

Terrorism: The use of violence, especially murder and bombing, in order to achieve political goals or to force a government to do something.

Unscrupulous: If you describe a person as unscrupulous, you are critical of the fact that they are prepared to act in a dishonest or immoral way to get what they want.

Definition Source:

COBUILD Advanced English Dictionary. Copyright © HarperCollins Publishers

About the Author

James A. DeMeo, M.S. has over 27 years in the security industry and is considered a subject matter expert in Event Security by several leading international and domestic magazines; Security Magazine, Security Management Magazine, and Pan Stadia. Mr. DeMeo earned his M.S. degree in Sport Management from Adelphi University in 2012. He was part of the AEG Leadership Team which opened the Barclays Center in 2012 (Brooklyn, New York).

Mr. DeMeo participated as an integral component of a research team including esteemed professors for a poster project presented at the North American Society for Sport Management Conference (NASSM, June 4th, 2016, Orlando, FL) entitled, "*Professional Sport Security and Marketing Interface: A Delphi Study, 'Assessing the Influence of Sport Security Operations on the Guest Experience: Using the Delphi Method to Understand Practitioner Perspectives,'*" later published in *The Journal of Sport Safety* (The University of Southern Mississippi).

He has delivered presentations at several national conferences and has spoken at numerous colleges and universities throughout the U.S. on sport security operations. Mr. DeMeo is the Founder, President, and CEO of USESC (Unified Sports and Entertainment Security Consulting, LLC; smeventsecurity.com). His company is based in Raleigh, North Carolina.

On September 1, 2017, Mr. DeMeo was recognized and honored by Security Magazine as one of The Most Influential People in Security, 2017. Past award recipients have included top corporate CSO's, CISO's as well as individuals such as Senator Joseph Lieberman, Representative Michael Rogers, Judge William Webster, FBI Director Robert Mueller, and INTERPOL Security General Ronald Noble.

Acknowledgments

Writing my very first book was a challenge on many fronts. Without the help, assistance, guidance, encouragement, and mentorship of some very talented individuals in my life, I would not have been able to complete this work. I want to offer a heartfelt special thank you to the following people who have become a part of my life and have helped me along my journey.

Special thanks to my family and friends, Michelle Hill, Victoria Freudiger, Michael Scott, Capt. Jacques Gilbert, Frank Bussey, Felix Nater, Kurt Jordan, Andy Jabbour, Stephen Coolahan, Dr. Tim Rice, Dr. Anthony Franklin, Terry Waldrop, Anthony Speroni, Jeannette Collins, Cody Mulla, A.D./Capt. Raymond J. Hughes, Dr. Greg Letter, Robert "Justice" Narvaez, Terry Goldstein, Dan Bedard, Diane Ritchey, Claire Meyer, Katie McIntyre, Michael D'Angelo, Ret. Lt. Robert Sputo, D/Sgt. Carlo Maltempi, Patrick Daly, Fr. Ranjan Cletus, and the late Robert Sena.

What's YOUR Plan?

If, somehow, I have not mentioned you, my sincerest apologies. I will make every effort to do so in my next book on Event Security.

Thank You

James A. DeMeo, MS

> Be true to yourself, help others, make each day your masterpiece, make friendship a fine art, drink deeply from good books – especially the Bible, build a shelter against a rainy day, give thanks for your blessings and pray for guidance every day.
>
> ~John Wooden

How to Order

To purchase bulk orders for your school, business, association, and other groups, or to book Mr. DeMeo to speak at your next event:

Email: jdemeo65@gmail.com

Website: smeeventsecurity.com

References

Chapter 1:

1. Department of Homeland Security research reveals that the average duration of an active shooter incident at a school is 12.5 minutes. In contrast, the average response time for law enforcement is 18 minutes. Oct 16, 2013

2. Quicker Response to Active Shooters - Article - POLICE Magazine

   www.policemag.com/channel/patrol/articles/.../quicker-response-to-active-shooters.aspx

3. https://nrf.com/news/partners-prevention

Chapter 3:

1. https://www.churchsecurityalliance.com/texas-churches-now-allowed-to-have-own-armed-security-teams/

Chapter 4:

1. https://www.dhs.gov/xlibrary/assets/active_shooter_booklet.pdf

2. https://www.hklaw.com/publications/the-new-fbi-study-on-active-shooters-is-your-workplace-safe-02-02-2015/

Chapter 5:

1. http://www.harvard.edu/harvard-glance

2. http://www.forbes.com/sites/caranewlon/2014/07/31/the-college-amenities-arms-race/

3. NCS4.com

4. http://www.athleticbusiness.com/recreation-outdoor-security/student-makes-bomb-threat-at-wsu-rec-center.html

Chapter 7:

1. http://abcnews.go.com/US/back-aurora-colorado-movie-theater-shooting-years/story?id=48730066

2. http://www.natoonline.org/resources/training/

3. AMC Theatre Code of Conduct:

https://cdn.amctheatres.com/Media/Default/PDFs/code-of-conduct-policy.pdf

Chapter 8:

1. http://www.athleticbusiness.com/rec-center/survey-reveals-security-practices-at-public-recreation-centers.html

2. http://bgr.com/2017/03/07/columbine-shooting-dylan-klebold-mother-ted-talk/